# How to be a Self-Made Millionaire

*What Are the Secrets of Success?*

*Cliff K. Locks*

Serial Entrepreneur
Executive and Life Coach

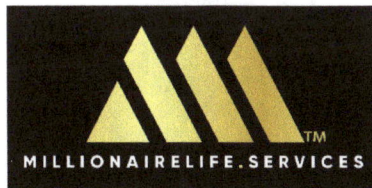

MILLIONAIRELIFE.SERVICES

https://MillionaireLife.Services

# Dedication

*To our wonderful children, fine students of life, who are caring, kind, loving, and giving individuals, who bring out the best in others.*

# Copyright Page

*Info@MillionaireLife.Services*

*© 2023 Millionaire Life Services*

*ISBN: 979-8-9864571-4-7*

# Forward

In the pursuit of wealth and financial success, there is a common dream shared by many: to become a self-made millionaire. This aspiration isn't just about accumulating money; it's about attaining a level of financial freedom and security that allows you to live life on your terms. It's a dream of self-reliance, accomplishment, and the realization of one's full potential.

In "Self-Made Millionaire: What Are the Secrets of Success?" we embark on a journey to uncover the principles and strategies that can help transform this dream into reality. Through the pages of this book, we will explore the stories of individuals who started with nothing but a vision and determination and ultimately achieved millionaire status through their hard work, perseverance, and strategic thinking.

The table of contents provides a roadmap for our exploration, with each chapter delving into a specific aspect of the self-made millionaire's journey. From dreaming bigger to embracing self-discipline, from nurturing creativity to valuing integrity, and from the importance of physical health to the relentless pursuit of your goals, this book will offer valuable insights and practical advice to help you on your path to financial success.

Throughout these pages, you'll discover that the road to becoming a self-made millionaire is not just about money; it's about personal growth, resilience, and the willingness to continuously learn and adapt. The stories and lessons shared within will inspire you to take control of your financial destiny, regardless of your current circumstances or background.

Whether you're just starting your journey or you're already on the path to financial success, "Self-Made Millionaire: What Are the Secrets of Success?" will serve as a valuable guide, offering wisdom, motivation, and a blueprint for achieving your financial goals.

As you turn the pages and absorb the insights within, remember that the journey to becoming a self-made millionaire is not a sprint but a marathon. It requires dedication, focus, and the willingness to learn from both successes and setbacks. So, let's begin this journey together, armed with the knowledge and inspiration needed to unlock your potential and attain the financial success you desire.

Dream big, stay focused, and never stop believing in yourself.

I look forward to taking this journey with you.

Cliff K. Locks

# Table of Contents

# Introduction

Our world is witnessing the greatest surge of first-generation millionaires we have ever seen. These individuals often had humble beginnings, but through desire, vision, hard work, and resilience, we have witnessed how they have amassed great wealth for themselves and their families. Indeed, we live in a world filled with possibilities like never before. We live in an era where the opportunities to amass wealth are everywhere.

The good news is that everyone, including you, can partake in those opportunities. You can be wealthy, regardless of your background or present reality. About now, you are probably wondering how. Here's the how: through desire, vision, hard work, and persistence, you can accumulate more wealth than you ever thought possible.

A million-and-one questions have been asked about self-made millionaires, especially what they do that others do not. Inquiring minds are curious to know what secrets, knowledge, qualities, and skills they possess. Others want to know just about everything that may contribute to a self-made millionaire's ability to cross over from poverty and obscurity to wealth and significance. They want to know what makes these individuals the exception.

If you have asked these questions about the success of self-made millionaires, this book is for you. Throughout the following pages, you'll find the answers. This book was written from an in-depth study of the practices of more than one thousand first-generation millionaires in the United States. We understand that the best way to attain true success and financial freedom is to devote one's life to learning what other wealthy people have done. With that passion for learning, you must commit yourself to emulate the qualities of highly successful people.

This book is all about teaching you the ancient secrets of first-generation success, the principles that have helped so many people move from poverty and insignificance to wealth and affluence in one generation. I will prove that most self-made millionaires became successful primarily because of their perseverance. Their success was not due to money. Instead, it was the individual qualities they possessed and the skills they developed along the way. These critical keys allowed them to make money and maintain it.

There are an estimated 15,298,070 millionaire households in the United States. That's 11.89% of all households in our country. Multimillionaires with more than 3 million in net worth are roughly 6.25%, and deca-millionaires, households with 10 million or more in net worth, are 1.13%. To be considered the top percent of millionaires in the U.S., an individual has to make just over 11 million now.[1]

The data points to perseverance as one quality that they all possessed. Every individual with a genuine desire for wealth must first understand that success is not easy and never will be. It comes at the cost of serious devotion and hard work. One will encounter failure and rejection, and despite this, you must muster the courage to practice relentless perseverance in the face of all this.

You will learn that all of this and more are the price successful people pay to attain the results that we admire and strive to achieve today. The laws of the universe are immutable even in the pursuit of financial freedom. Indeed, "what we sow is what we reap."

As per this Law of Cause and Effect, anyone, including you, can indeed be successful. Regardless of race, gender, ethnicity, or background, if you learn and follow the path of successful people, you can also experience success. The secrets will be demystified for you on every page and paragraph of this book. Remember three words because they will be critical to your success: learn, grow, and become.

I look forward to taking this journey with you.

---

[1] *How many millionaires are there in America?* DQYDJ. (2021, July 10). Retrieved April 20, 2022, from https://dqydj.com/how-many-millionaires-decamillionaires-america/

# 1

# **Dream Bigger**

Do you think you have big dreams? If you answered yes, you still need to dream bigger. Success is indeed for the dreamers who dare to achieve their goals with passion, courage, and perseverance. I know this because every millionaire studied possessed the ability to create things first with the power of their imagination before bringing them to reality. This is true for anyone who has ever attained success in any endeavor, whether in sports, business, academics, technology, etc.

Because this is true, it's only fair to say that success in any endeavor can only be achieved if it was first conceived in your imagination. If you genuinely desire to be a millionaire, allow yourself to dream of owning millions of dollars. Picture the way you want to act and the things you would love to do. The funny thing is that it costs nothing to dream. Dream and look deep within yourself. Then, observe what it feels like.

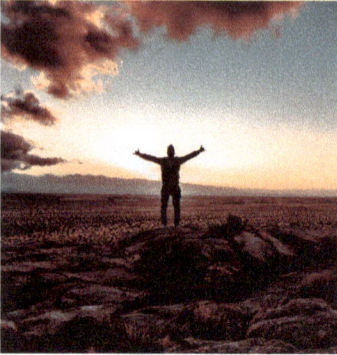

### Allow Yourself to Dream

Because this is true, it's only fair to say that success in any endeavor can only be achieved if
it was first conceived in your imagination.

Having such a long-range vision will be the source of the motivation you will need. It will provide positivity and determination so that even when you experience inevitable setbacks, you are reassured and fired up by the vision you have set for yourself. And do not be mistaken: setbacks will occur. Setbacks are part of your journey to success, so that long-range vision will be vital in keeping you on your path.

If your "why" is strong enough, there is no "how" that can be too great. Read that again, and then let that truth set in for a moment. With that thought in mind, write down everything you would like to do or accomplish if success were a given.

**Start With WHY**

If your "why" is strong enough, there is no "how" that can be too great. Read that again, and then let that truth set in for a moment. With that thought in mind, write down everything you would like to do or accomplish if success were a given. Then, choose to work on one after the other, in order of priority, and get to work every day to bring it alive.

Then, choose to work on one after the other, in order of priority, and get to work every day to bring it alive. Be sure to check off each accomplishment along the way. This will continue to work as momentum to remind you how that strong "why" makes anything possible.

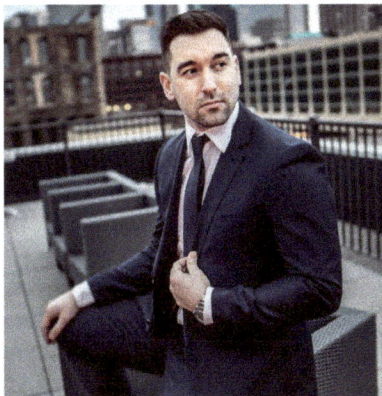

To achieve your goals, start envisioning them in your mind daily. Use your imagination, desire, and will. You will find a way to bring it to reality by doing this. Remember: A vision backed with informed action is the most powerful force for success in every human endeavor, particularly financial freedom. Keep dreaming. Keep winning.

# 2

## Focus All the Way

Two important factors determine our outcome in life. One is what we think about most of the time, and the other is the emotions sparked by those thoughts. The Law of Concentration iterates that everything you are and that you have today was formed from those things you have concentrated your thought and attention on over the past few years. It also predicts that your outcome in the next phase of your life will be primarily determined by what you concentrate your mind and attention on today. Only you can decide exactly what you want to see in every aspect of life for the next few weeks, months, and, yes, even years ahead.

Now, consider the various aspects of your life. This includes your finances, career, business, relationships, family, spirituality, health, personal development, and education, etc. It will help if you start by writing down the specific goals you wish to accomplish in each area of your life. Be sure to assign a timeline in which you choose to reach your goals. This is an essential step in the process that cannot be neglected. If it's a big goal, you may decide to break it into smaller parts. This will enhance your concentration and allows you to focus on the detail of each task.

**Two important factors determine our outcome in life**

**1. What we think about most of the time**

2. Emotions sparked by those thoughts.

The Law of Concentration iterates that everything you are and that you have today was formed from those things you have concentrated your thought and attention on over the past few years.

Because financial freedom is a priority, place your financial goals at the top of your list. Write down everything you would need to do to accomplish these goals.

**Consider the various aspects of your life.**

This includes your:

| | | | |
|---|---|---|---|
| 01 | Finances | 06 | Spirituality |
| 02 | Career | 07 | Health |
| 03 | Business | 08 | Personal Dev |
| 04 | Relationships | 09 | Education |
| 05 | Family | | |

## Prioritize Financial Freedom

Because financial freedom is a priority, place your financial goals at the top of your list.

01   Write down everything you would need to do to accomplish these goals.

02   Organize these goals into smaller objectives, including daily and weekly tasks that will ultimately bring you closer to your goals.

03   Convert these objectives into a workable action plan by specifying the when, the where, and how for each task.

Next, you need to organize these goals into smaller objectives, including daily and weekly tasks that will ultimately bring you closer to your goals.

Convert these objectives into a workable action plan by specifying the when, the where, and how for each task. Now, get to work on it immediately. Do what you can every day and see yourself speedily moving closer to all you desire.

Remember, the more focused attention you place on your goals, the closer you move towards them. This is the power that your brain holds. Success requires a single-minded level of attention to your goals, discipline, and perseverance. And it requires you to prioritize other things that do not fall within your goals. You need to organize your list of priorities, including work, family, and any outside interests. This is the price everyone must pay for success, including every self-made millionaire in the world today.

The more focused attention you place on your goals, the closer you move towards them.

This is the power that your brain holds. Success requires a single-minded level of attention to your goals, discipline, and perseverance. And it requires you to prioritize other things that do not fall within your goals.

You must choose a path and stick to it. In our world of multi-verities, distractions, and confusion, if you are not ready to choose a direction in life and stick to it with laser focus, success may be far beyond your reach. Your dedication to your goals will pay off big time once you start reaching them. But you must stick to those goals and focus all the way.

**You must choose a path and stick to it.**

# 3

## Take Charge

The attitude of many people who don't succeed is the failure to take on full responsibility. Instead, they push it onto others. Many of us go through life blaming our parents, the government, our boss, the economy, and everyone but ourselves for our situation. You will learn that true success begins from taking absolute responsibility for your destiny because it's your destiny. Your future. If it is to be successful, then it's up to you to make it happen!

Until you fully take responsibility for your present situation, you will never find the courage or muscle the energy you need to move forward. You must learn the lessons now and take bold steps to enter your next level. Remember, you own your life; take responsibility for your life.

There is one thing I have found to be common to every self-made millionaire, and it is the understanding that "only they" can be responsible for their success. Nobody else will do, what you should do for yourself. Everything that leads to success begins with holding yourself accountable for your own life. You are your biggest ally or your own worst enemy; only you can choose which one you will be.

This is true for every aspect of your life. If you do not like your job, credit, and financial situation, it is your responsibility to change it. If you do not like your body shape or health situation, it is your responsibility to learn what it takes and then act immediately to modify it. You must take up the mindset that you are self-employed, the president of "You" Corporation. Take action now and stop waiting for anyone else to change your situation because only you can.

The attitude of many people who don't succeed is the failure to take on full responsibility. Instead, they push it onto others.

## Hold Yourself
**Accountable**

## It is Your
**Responsibility**

# 4

## Love is a Must

From the beginning of time, man thrived in the areas in which he had strength and interest. It would be best to go all out, find what you enjoy doing, determine your areas of power, and find a purpose, a mission, in the fields of your abilities. When you have this purpose and mission in place, you will find you are driven to succeed at what you have set out to do, and you will accomplish it.

True wealth does not just come from merely wishing for it. It comes from the passion, mission, and enterprise to drive that goal with the fuel of enthusiasm and strength. Passion and strength are vital ingredients to happiness.

Perhaps your present career is not fulfilling. It is imperative to check your levels of happiness and satisfaction. It would help if you thought about how passionate you are about your job. If you don't find yourself to be passionate about this job, ask yourself if you can create a spark so that you are happy. You may find that you need to search for the job you want and pursue your dreams. Happiness in what you choose to do all day is so important.

**Find a Purpose**
In Your Fields

Some facts point to the importance of loving what you do to bring about success. Your success in any endeavor is directly proportional to your love level. For example, the higher your love level, the higher your chances of success. The higher your success, the higher your love level is in return.

This is because genuine passion sparks up the energy and motivation to perform at the optimum level all the time. This quality of performance is what guarantees success. Success and repeated success also translate to even greater passion. For example, the more you succeed at something, your energy level is increased for you to do even more.

Genuine passion sparks up the energy and motivation to perform at the optimum level all the time.

When choosing a path for your life, remember that your success will always be hinged on your passion. If you lack passion where your work is concerned, your work will suffer. You may decide to do what you love or choose to love what you do in the end, but either way, passion and love are a must. Being mindful in choosing our path is important.

Success will always be hinged on your Passion.

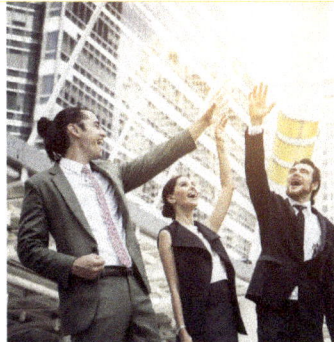

# 5

## Work, Work, Don't Stop

When it comes to success, a fact that can never be overemphasized is that there is no alternative to hard work. There just isn't. I have never met any successful individual who was not a workaholic in business, career, or any other endeavor. If your goal is to attain a level of success in life, particularly in the area of your finances, then you must be ready to work hard. Be prepared to work hard and be willing to work long enough until your aspirations become your reality.

Success comes to those who work hard.

Another character trait in every self-made millionaire studied is that they showed up early every day, worked hard and long, and stayed later than everyone else. They commit their entire life and energy to drive their mission through enterprise and ultimately attain an enviable level of financial success.

Hence, if your goal is to become a millionaire, you need to understand that success has no place for laziness. Either you'll put one hundred percent of your effort into what you do every day, or you will not get to where you want to go. The price for success is not negotiable; it must be paid in full and in advance. The price is work, more work, and hard work. Success will be far beyond your reach until you are committed to working harder and longer than everyone else in the game. Grasping this truth is essential to attain your dreams.

Start each new day with new energy, as success is a reward for high-value productivity-driven people. They work 100% of the time but leave room for creative thinking and exchanging ideas with others while at work.

A think tank can be instrumental in bringing in fresh thoughts and new insights and, therefore, new energy and passion to each day. Energy and passion are vital to success.

**Showed up early everyday**
**Worked hard and long**

Successful people do not define their work or measure success just by activity. They focus on productivity and learn every day to channel all their efforts and energy into the most productive activities that are best worthy of their time and energy. This is wisdom that each person seeking wealth needs to understand. Working hard and long every day can help you achieve your goals. There is no alternative to hard work.

**Energy and Passion**
**are vital to success.**

# 6

# Get Hungry for Knowledge

Some have millions because they have the knowledge, and they practice what they have learned. You must seek knowledge, the *right* knowledge. Upon this realization, you can begin to seek out the knowledge you are missing that will move you towards success. You will be able to seek out success itself.

**The problem is not In the availability of knowledge.**

When it comes to success, the principles are universal. The knowledge of these principles is dispersed in pages of hundreds of books globally today. It can be found, but you must be a person who is hungry enough to seek it.

When it comes to closing the knowledge gap between the rich and the poor, the problem is not in the availability of knowledge. This knowledge is not some secret code

31

hidden in a tome from some ancient civilization; the knowledge we seek is available everywhere. It is in the books you need to read, the audiobooks you should listen to, and the teachings of men and women who have demonstrated this knowledge to various degrees. They have reached great heights and passed it on through several generations.

**You have got to be**
Hungry for knowledge.

You have got to be hungry for knowledge. You have to seek and learn what wealthy people have shared. Then, you may be able to practice what successful people have done and accomplish what they have accomplished. You can receive a similar result in life. But you must continually have a hunger for knowledge and dedicate yourself to learning the secrets of success.

Here are some quick tips on developing a habit for continual learning:

1. Commit one hour every day to reading something on success.

2.  Maximize your commuting time by listening to podcasts and audio training while driving to and from work.
3.  Attend Zoom workshops and seminars that you consider relevant to your field.

**Developing a habit for continual learning:**

Success requires mastery. This mastery can only be attained by acquiring relevant and timely knowledge in your field. Get hungry for knowledge.

**Success Requires Mastery**

This mastery can only be attained by acquiring relevant and timely knowledge in your field. **Get hungry for knowledge.**

# 7

## Pay Yourself First

Making money is not the most challenging thing in business; learning how to keep it and growing it is. Again, you must pay yourself first. I'm sure you must have heard the phrase "pay yourself first" a couple of times, and it is vital if your goal is to accrue a lot of wealth and build a sustainable enterprise. There are important reasons why you should do this.

First, paying yourself helps you stay in charge of your business or personal finances. You can start simply by committing to save at least 10% of everything you earn. When you practice this goal long enough, it becomes a habit. It becomes the very seeds of success.

Saving money requires a tremendous level of discipline. This is especially true in a world where irrelevant commodities have been flaunted at you every day through mainstream media outlets and social media. Still, until you commit yourself to developing the required discipline to save and multiply money, true success remains out of reach.

**Saving money requires a tremendous level of Discipline.**

Making money is just one step to wealth accumulation, but it takes the discipline to save and reinvest your money to multiply your wealth. The wealthiest people are not just people who work to earn money, but they also put their money to work for them. They put their money to work through various investment vehicles. All this begins with exerting the discipline to save a part of everything you earn.

**Making money is just one step to wealth accumulation**

I cannot find anyone who does not prioritize savings and investment in all my studies and interaction with self-made millionaires. Hence, if your top goal is to accumulate wealth, you need to practice this discipline to pay yourself first. You then must reinvest into your business and reinvest in yourself above all else.

Every self-made millionaire acquired the discipline required to delay immediate gratification and pleasure. They carefully and logically consider their buying decisions.

**Delay immediate gratification and pleasure.**

They are not impulsive buyers who are compelled by emotions. No matter what they earn or what they want, they have created a habit that drives them to save at least 10% of all they earn, and so should you. Without such discipline, wealth acquisition is just a fantasy beyond any man's reach.

Save at least 10% of everything you earn.

# 8

## Add More Value

Self-made millionaires are always looking for better ways to deliver value to their customers. Money gravitates towards value, meaning that the more value you can add to your customers and industry, the more money you make. When it comes to success in business, you must first improve on the value you provide, and the reward will follow.

**Money gravitates**
**Towards value**

Let us think about the value this way: if you choose from two or more business offers, your choice would probably be based on price. You'll look at which one offers the best value for the price. Quality is critical in decision-making. You will choose which one provides superior quality. Speed of delivery and convenience, who delivers when promised, and who makes it convenient and easy to work with will all be questions you should consider. These are some vital factors that self-made millionaires consider during their strategy sessions.

**Quality is critical in Decision-making.**

They continually strive to offer products with superior value in price, quality, speed, convenience, and more. Therefore, they deliver more value in the marketplace and gain an excellent reputation to continually grow their business. Being sure always to present a superior value to your customers is necessary. Having these priorities present offers a path toward success and wealth.

Develop a reputation for being the most reliable in your field. When someone needs to get the best results in the shortest possible time, be the person they call. Embrace the motto, "Do it faster, do it better!" This will ensure you are competitive in your industry and contribute to your financial success.

To develop a reputation for superior quality, you should under promise and over-deliver. Find ways to impress your customers regularly. Once you accomplish that, you will find that it is your brand that readily comes to their mind first. It will build brand awareness for others, and your business will thrive.

**Find ways to impress your customers regularly.**

To develop a reputation for superior quality, you should under promise and over-deliver.

Develop a reputation for quality and convenience. People in this age and time choose the top service among many alternatives in the services and products industry. Whatever you do, ensure that customer service and satisfaction are always a priority.

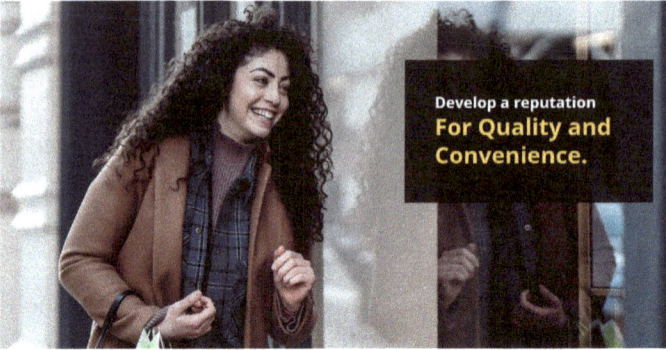

Develop a reputation
**For Quality and Convenience.**

# 9

## Develop a Reputation for Integrity and Strive for Excellence

Stay true to yourself and others. Say what you do and do what you say. These should be two things that you embrace and practice in business and life. As young entrepreneurs starting in life and business, we often underplay the value of integrity. Integrity is the currency, indeed the only currency upon which you can build a sustainable and robust brand.

**Stay true to**
Yourself and others.

Without the required trust capital, no one will be willing to commit their time and resources to you. More than any other endeavor, business success demands that you build a reputation for complete honesty. Be known to stay true to yourself and others, always.

**Build a reputation for Complete Honesty.**

If you desire to create a viable business and accumulate wealth like most self-made millionaires, you must pay attention to trust. For without trust, there is no hope for business success. The more people trust you, the more they commit their resources to you. The more they are willing to work with you and for you, the more they recognize you and your product.

You must learn to strive for excellence, always. Whatever path you have chosen for success, you must commit to excellence in every way. The reason is straightforward: everybody is attracted to excellence. Your customers, investors, workers, and everybody involved in your business process will not only expect this from you but be drawn to it. The more attention you pay to excellence, the more drawn people will be to you and your business.

**Strive for Excellence,**

Success demands that you strive to be among the top 10% in your industry. It requires that you become exceptionally competent at whatever you do. You need to be the most knowledgeable person in your field. You need to be the go-to guy when a solution is required in your field.

Remember, if you desire true success in life and business, integrity and excellence are core values that you can never afford to compromise on. These values must be deeply ingrained into you. They must be part of what drives you and sets you apart from other competitors in your field.

**Be the go-to guy**

Success demands that you strive to be among the top 10% in your industry. It requires that you become exceptionally competent at whatever you do.

## Remember

**If you desire true success in life and business, integrity and excellence are core values that you can never afford to compromise on.**

These values must be deeply ingrained into you. They must be part of what drives you and sets you apart from other competitors in your field.

# 10

## Self-discipline Is a Must

You need to understand this tremendous truth: discipline is the fundamental force that drives every tangible human accomplishment. Without it, every other success principle is defeated. The process that leads to success requires tremendous discipline. You have to be willing to do this to obtain success.

**Understand this**
**tremendous truth:**
Discipline is the fundamental force that drives every tangible human accomplishment.

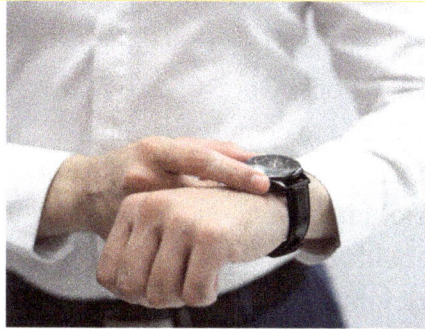

First, to determine what you need to do to get your desired result, it takes discipline to set intelligent and informed goals for achieving your desired outcome. But most importantly, it takes discipline to get into focused action every day to bring your dreams alive. That's probably the most challenging aspect of discipline that people struggle to commit to. You must rise every morning to put your feet on the floor, ready to tackle the day's challenges.

The journey to financial freedom is laced with many distractions. Once you have determined precisely what you need to do to reach your desired outcome, achieving it requires tremendous discipline. It also includes the determination to do what you should do, when you should do it, regardless of the distractions. Self-discipline is necessary and it's difficult to accomplish big things if you are distracted by small things.

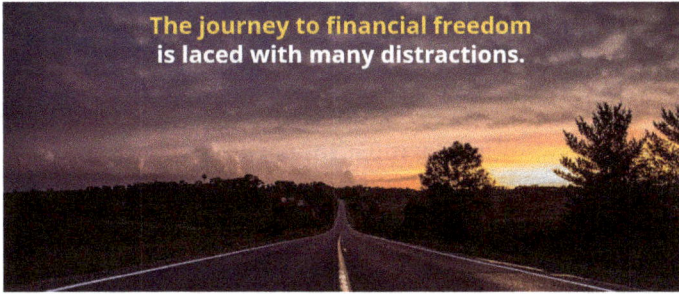
The journey to financial freedom is laced with many distractions.

Your ability to keep yourself in check every day and commit to your goals with laser focus is indeed what guarantees success. Discipline is self-control, self-mastery, self-direction, and delayed gratification. It involves avoiding temporary pleasure for long-term gains. Discipline is your ability to continually pursue positive outcomes rather than easy shortcuts continuously. Discipline is your ability to stay true to your pursuit in the face of all distractions.

**Discipline is**
**Self-control**

Discipline is your ability to stay true to your pursuit in the face of all distractions.

If your goal is to become a self-made millionaire, you must know that discipline is necessary. Discipline is difficult, but it is possible. Discipline is challenging, but the lack of discipline is more challenging. When it comes to attaining financial freedom, discipline is not negotiable. Starting today, begin to practice self-discipline and mastery in various aspects of your life because discipline is a must for success.

**Discipline is Necessary.**

Discipline is difficult, but it is possible. Discipline is challenging, but the lack of discipline is more challenging. When it comes to attaining financial freedom, discipline is not negotiable.

# 11

# Unlock Your Creative Genius

There is a creative genius inside of you trying to find a way to express brilliance. Please let it. You must understand that creative thinking is a critical part of your wealth creation journey, and you will need to unlock your creative genius to succeed. You will meet your share of challenges and persevere to find the solutions. Your creative ability relies on your innate giftedness and your continuous improvement through learning.

**Unlock Your**
**Creative Genius**

There is a creative genius inside of you trying to find a way to express brilliance. *Please let it.*

Your ability to innovate and offer creative solutions grows substantially by continuously improving yourself. Again, this is where discipline comes into play. You must be committed to giving your best effort every single day.

**Give your best effort every single day.**

Your ability to innovate and offer creative solutions grows substantially by continuously improving yourself. Again, this is where discipline comes into play. You must be committed to giving your best effort every single day.

Almost every part of the business process requires a level of creativity. This includes your business modeling, marketing approach, product design, systems, and structure, branding, and continuous innovations. Hence, you must constantly tap into your creative genius to offer innovative solutions.

**Creative Genius**

Almost every part of the business process requires a level of creativity.

You will learn the value of thinking fast and taking action. Self-made millionaires are highly decisive and action-driven. They think fast, thoroughly examine the situation, and quickly ascertain what steps need to be implemented. They back up that decision with the corresponding action. They are solution-driven people, not problem-driven, so they commit their time and energy to activities that enhance their decision-making skills. Such activities primarily involve acquiring adequate information on their business' hyper-specific details and then getting a well-rounded understanding of the challenges to enable them to make informed decisions.

**Learn the value of thinking fast and taking action.**

Self-made millionaires are highly decisive and action-driven. They think fast, thoroughly examine the situation, and quickly ascertain what steps need to be implemented. They back up that decision with the corresponding action.

Ensure you obtain feedback on different aspects of your business and make necessary corrections. The truth is that ideas do not come fully formed. You must be ready to create, recreate, and innovate as you go along. Do not hesitate to ask for advice from people you admire and trust. If you do not have connections to those people, reach out to your LinkedIn network to find them.

**Obtain feedback** **different aspects of your business and make necessary corrections.**

The truth is that ideas do not come fully formed. You must be ready to create, recreate, and innovate as you go along.

It's becoming easier to collaborate with outside experts, to help CEOs, Executives, Entrepreneurs, and Boards to obtain the needed resources to scale their companies. Please view the resource page at the end of this book; you'll have access to personalized one-on-one executive coaching, board advisor, and mentor-driven programs.

**Collaborate with Outside Experts**
It's becoming easier to collaborate with outside experts, to help CEOs, Executives, Entrepreneurs, and Boards to obtain the needed resources to scale their companies.

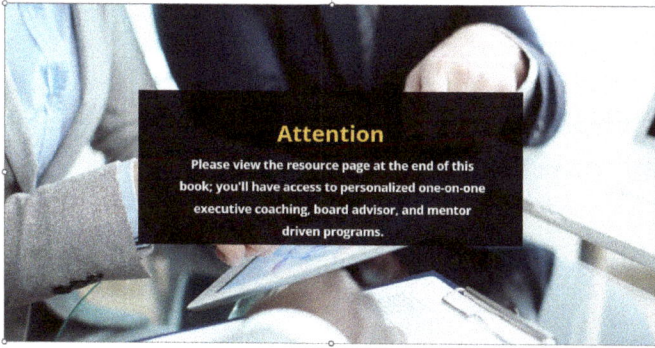

**Attention**

Please view the resource page at the end of this book; you'll have access to personalized one-on-one executive coaching, board advisor, and mentor driven programs.

# 12

# Locate Likeminded People and Stick with Them

Whether negative or positive, you are the sum of the people and places you surround yourself with. You must surround yourself with positive, like-minded people who can add real value to your life and enhance your pursuit of success. Be deliberate about the people you allow in your inner circle; ensure you stay away from negative minded people. People who are always complaining can become toxic people. As discussed below, there are three major categories of people that constitute a positive inner circle.

**Surround yourself with**
**Positive, like-minded people**

Whether negative or positive, you are the sum of the people and places you surround yourself with. You must surround yourself with positive, like-minded people who can add real value to your life and enhance your pursuit of success.

Be deliberate about the people you allow in your inner circle; ensure you stay away from negative minded people. People who are always complaining can become toxic people. As discussed below, there are three major categories of people that constitute a positive inner circle.

First, it is the people you admire. Call them mentors or coaches, but these are the people who have been where you want to go. They have acquired the kind of wealth or other results you desire to obtain. Their presence in your life inspires you to strive for more, believe more, learn more, do more, and be more. It would be best if you had them in your life, making a positive impact.

**1. The People You Admire**

Call them mentors or coaches, but these are the people who have been where you want to go.

The second set of people are the people you are presently on the same level with. These are other people like yourself who are equally hungry and highly motivated for a change. These people have the character, creativeness, and drive to get the results you admire and that you would love to emulate. They are people you can comfortably and safely share ideas and inspire each other to pursue your vision.

**2. The people you are <u>presently</u> on the same level with**

These are other people like yourself who are equally hungry and highly motivated for a change.

There are also the people you choose to mentor going forward. The best way to establish yourself is to pass the lessons you have learned along the journey on to others. As you move from point A to B to pursue success, ensure you do all you can to help others, following after you. Help inspire them with your knowledge and lessons. Paying it forward is a good way to look at it. They are your co-travelers on your journey toward success, and their ideas, drive, and creativity should constitute a significant part of your circle.

**3. The people <u>you choose</u> to mentor going forward.**

There are also the people The best way to establish yourself is to pass the lessons you have learned along the journey on to others.

If you have people in your life that are draining you and not adding any real value to your life, then it may be time for you to reevaluate these relationships. This is particularly important because you are the total of the people and places you surround yourself with, whether negative or positive. When you surround yourself with positive people, you will be positive. If you surround yourself with negative people, you can begin to feel negative. The choice is always yours, and you may keep certain people in your life because they are family or long-term friends.

**Reevaluate**
**Your relationships**

If you have people in your life that are draining you and not adding any real value to your life, then it may be time for you to reevaluate these relationships.

Try to surround yourself with positive people and keep the negative people at a distance if you can. That does not mean cutting off ties with long-term people you have a relationship with. We are talking about implementing boundaries.

Positive people often try to change the thinking of negative thinking people. It is exceedingly rare that you can change someone's outlook on life. They must want to change, to be a positive, forward-thinking person. If you have relationships with negative people, consider carefully how much time and influence you allow these people to have on your behavior and set necessary boundaries with those people. Do not spend excessive time trying to change them, just move forward. You make your own positivity in life. Remember to find the people your future self wants to associate with and make them a part of your present life now.

## Implementing
## boundaries.

Positive people often try to change the thinking of negative thinking people. It is exceedingly rare that you can change someone's outlook on life.

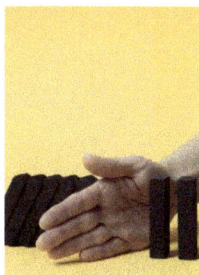

### Consider Your Time

If you have relationships with negative people, consider carefully how much time and influence you allow these people to have on your behavior.

### Do not spend excessive time

Just move forward. You make your own positivity in life. Remember to find the people your future self wants to associate with and make them a part of your present life now.

# 13

## Never Ignore Your Physical Health

Health is wealth. Success requires a high level of work and energy, which only a healthy person will have. You must take to heart this vital fact when it comes to success and the role your health will play in it. It is crucial to pay keen attention to the state of your physical fitness on your way to financial freedom. A poor state of health can significantly hinder your wealth accumulation. I have never seen any man on a sickbed thinking of anything else other than to regain his health. After all, what use will your wealth be if you don't live long enough to enjoy it due to ill health?

**Health is** Wealth

**Pay attention to your physical fitness**

The food you eat has a significant impact on your health. A balanced diet is a meal that has every vital component needed for the human body's optimal functioning, and this is precisely what you need to maintain an excellent state of health. Discipline yourself to develop a healthy eating habit; eat healthy meals, more vegetables, fruits, and water. Avoid buying and eating junk food, including various processed foods that offer no benefit and can contribute to obesity. If your goal is to lose weight, you will need to exert the discipline required in diets and exercise to keep fit.

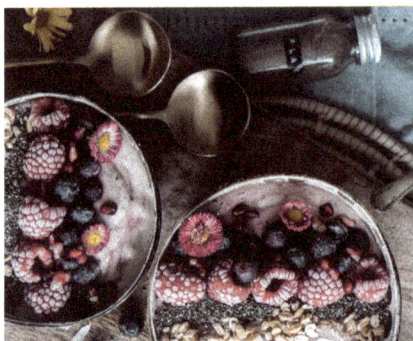

**A Balanced diet**

A balanced diet is a meal that has every vital component needed for the human body's optimal functioning, and this is precisely what you need to maintain an excellent state of health.

Exercise is a critical component of physical fitness. You do not need a rigorous routine like an athlete to keep fit. You can begin with a simple routine like taking a walk, jogging, running, or going for a swim, every morning.

**Exercise is a critical component of physical fitness.**

You do not need a rigorous routine like an athlete to keep fit. You can begin with a simple routine like taking a walk, jogging, running, or going for a swim, every morning.

Do some pushups, sit-ups, or planks. Yoga, meditation, and exercising a healthy mind are essential as well. Determine the routine that will help you attain your physical fitness and commit to it daily. Remember, physical fitness is never about how rigorous your exercise is; it is more about your level of consistency.

**Attain your**
**Physical fitness**

Do some pushups, sit-ups, or planks. Yoga, meditation, and exercising a healthy mind are essential as well. Determine the routine that will help you attain your physical fitness and commit to it daily.

Success requires that you dream big, work hard, and exert a significant level of discipline in everything you do. Never ignore your physical health because health, in and of itself, is wealth. Prioritize your physical health on your path towards wealth and success.

Success requires that you dream big, work hard, and exert a significant level of discipline in everything you do.

# 14

## Persistence is Key

Success is only reserved for the persistent when every other person has given up and conceded to defeat. The persistent person will push on with his last breath to earn the prize of success. When traveling the road to success, you must realize that it is not a straight line. It has many bumps along the journey. Some problematic situations would make many quit. However, the person who will be successful will take every hardship and obstacle and use it as a lever to get them to the next level.

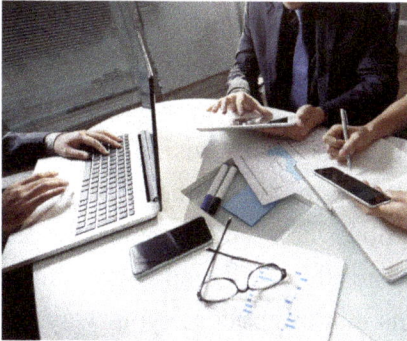

You can never **afford to give up.**

The ability to persist in the face of defeat is a vital requirement for any tangible accomplishment.

The ability to persist in the face of defeat is a vital requirement for any tangible accomplishment, particularly if you desire to accumulate wealth and become financially free. There will be some disappointments, setbacks, and serious hardship, but you can never afford to give up. Every setback in your pursuit of success is temporary, and if you persist long enough, you will find a way to break through them. Never give up.

**Success is only reserved for the persistent.**

The persistent person will push on with his last breath to earn the prize of success.

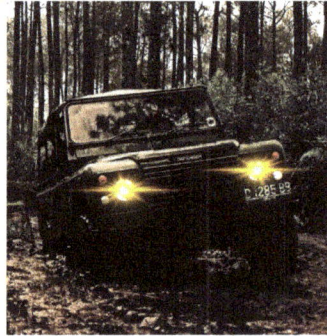

In preparing your mind for the difficult days, you must develop a long-range vision that is strong enough to help see you through every challenge because there will be several to overcome. When your "vision" is strong enough, there will not be any limitations you cannot overcome. Develop an obsession with your vision, plan for two to five years ahead; this will keep you confident in weathering the storms that might come your way.

## Develop a long-range vision

In preparing your mind for the difficult days, you must develop a long-range vision that is strong enough to help see you through every challenge because there will be several to overcome.

When your "vision" is strong enough, there will not be any limitations you cannot overcome. Develop an obsession with your vision, plan for two to five years ahead; this will keep you confident in weathering the storms that might come your way.

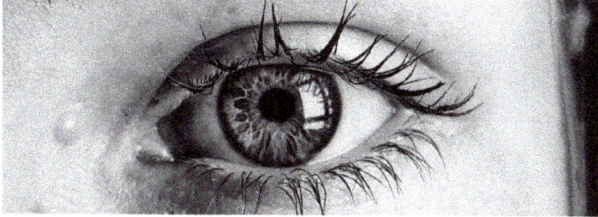

Tough days, disappointments, and setbacks are inevitable in business. All of these things are unfortunately guaranteed when striving for success. However, you must never forget that failure is never an option.

Fix your gaze on your goals, and never exercise any fear of failure. If anything, learn from the mistakes and vow to have them make you stronger, smarter, and more aware so that you can foresee them in advance when possible. When you reach those points when you want to throw the towel in and be done with your endeavors, you must force yourself to stick it out. No stinking thinking! Never give up!

**Failure is never an option.**
*Success is within you!*

Tough days, disappointments, and setbacks are inevitable in business. All of these things are unfortunately guaranteed when striving for success. However, you must never forget that failure is never an option.

Keep smiling and thinking positively. You can do this. I am here for you.

# Conclusion

By reading the previous pages, you now know that anyone can be successful, including you. Becoming a self-made millionaire is possible, but now you know the mysterious secret surrounding the mystery there is no real mystery. We all have it within us to do the hard work to experience financial freedom. But we must be committed to the journey, regardless of its challenges.

**Anyone can be successful including you.**

Becoming a self-made millionaire is possible, but now you know the mysterious secret surrounding the mystery there is no real mystery.

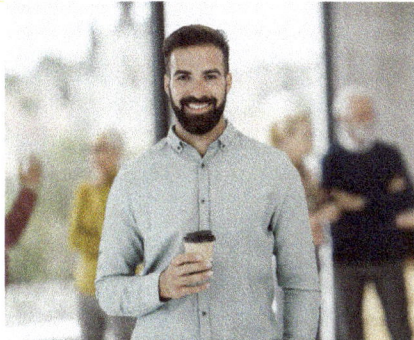

Through keeping our focus on our goals, practicing self-discipline, and continuing to be persistent, we can arrive at our destination: success. Financial freedom and wealth are big dreams but dreaming bigger and doing the hard work it takes means you can achieve whatever you set your mind to. Being open to constantly gaining the knowledge you need, surrounding yourself with like-minded individuals who share in your goals of reaching great heights, and practicing perseverance are part of this incredible journey.

You do not need to make this journey alone. Don't be afraid to ask for advice or seek a mentor who understands the path you are walking. A solid coach is part of a winning team, after all. I am here to help walk you through the challenges while seeking out wealth and working hard towards financial freedom. This book is just one part of that. Success is possible. Hard work is inevitable. But strength and persistence can make any dream, including wealth, a reality.

**You do not need to make this journey alone.**

Don't be afraid to ask for advice or seek a mentor who understands the path you are walking.

A solid coach is part of a winning team, after all. I am here to help walk you through the challenges while seeking out wealth and working hard towards financial freedom. This course is just one part of that. Success is possible. Hard work is inevitable. But strength and persistence can make any dream, including wealth, a reality.

Thank you so much for reading this book. I hope the advice I have strived to share with you has been helpful. It was once a goal for me, and now it is in your hands.

## Next Steps

Please Consider Our :

**Coaching membership program, where I will personally assist you on your journey to becoming a self-made millionaire.**

millionairelifeservices.uteach.io/membership

# Resources

Feel free to reach out and contact me. I welcome a confidential conversation about the most critical issues facing you, your family, and your business, including:

- Strategic planning toward your visions of success, goal setting, and building your Millionaire journey
- Career advancement and transition
- Planning, execution, and scaling a business
- Success is not an accident; it is purposeful planning and taking action
- Mentoring & depth of the executive bench
- Succession planning
- Mentoring & depth of the executive bench
- Values and life purpose
- Legacy and NetGen
- Kids and money
- Marriage and divorce
- Health concerns
- Values and life purpose
- Mentoring & depth of the executive bench
- Vacations and Retirement

To work together on your journey and continued success, visit our website at MillionaireLife.Services or choose a self-paced online course or membership plan at millionairelifeservices.uteach.io/courses

millionairelifeservices.uteach.io/membership

Our courses are designed to empower you with the knowledge and skills you need to achieve your goals.

*Cliff K. Locks*

*Serial Entrepreneur*

*Executive and Life Coach*

https://MillionaireLife.Services

# More Products by This Author

Elevate your path to success by discovering a range of valuable resources offered by this accomplished author. Explore a selection of books, self-paced courses, and exclusive coaching and mentoring programs designed to help you achieve your goals. Additionally, unlock the potential of joining an exclusive membership for high achievers to support you and your family on its successful journey to increased greatness and positive legacy. Don't miss out on the opportunity to take your success to the next level with the guidance and expertise of this accomplished author.

Other products by this author include:

*Please note that the publishing schedule will determine the availability of the printed books and Kindle edition, but all courses are currently accessible.*

1. Self-Made Millionaire: What Are the Secrets of Success? (Book you are currently reading)
2. 14 Secrets of Success to Become a Self-Made Millionaire (Course)
3. Key Strategies to Encourage Your Children to Succeed and Learn to Flourish Independently (Book and Course)

4. Guiding the Next Generation to Thrive and Build Continued Success for Your Family Legacy (Book and Course)
5. How to Achieve Success Fast - Learn How to Hit Goals by Harnessing the Power of Your Thoughts and Calculated Action (Book)
6. Achieving Success at an Accelerated Speed: Learn How to Hit Goals at Superhuman Speeds by Harnessing the Power of Thoughts and Calculated Actions (Course)
7. Mastering Anger: Understanding and Managing Your Emotions (Book and Course)
8. Emerging Leaders Program - The Basics and More for Becoming a Successful and Great Leader (Course)
9. Executive Leadership Academy - Practical Leadership Skills: Unlocking Your Full Potential (Course)
10. Millionaire Life Services Next Generation, Family, and Enterprise Executive Coaching (Membership)

*These books can be found on Amazon.com.*

*These courses and membership can be found on MillionaireLifeServices.uteach.io.*

*All courses are online and self-paced; pick up right where you left off and never lose your place with automatic progress tracking.*

www.ingramcontent.com/pod-product-compliance
Lightning Source LLC
Chambersburg PA
CBHW071248200326
41521CB00009B/1679